OLYMPIAD WORKBOOK

INTERNATIONAL ENGLISH OLYMPIAD

01 **Learning Objectives**

02 **Multiple Choice Questions**

03 **HOTS (Achievers Section)**

04 **Model Test Paper**

05 **Answer Keys and Solutions**

06 **OMR Answer Sheet**

V&S PUBLISHERS

Published by:

V&S PUBLISHERS

F-2/16, Ansari road, Daryaganj, New Delhi-110002
☎ 23240026, 23240027 • *Fax:* 011-23240028
✉ info@vspublishers.com • 🌐 www.vspublishers.com

Online Brandstore: amazon.in/vspublishers

Regional Office : Hyderabad

5-1-707/1, Brij Bhawan (Beside Central Bank of India Lane)
Bank Street, Koti, Hyderabad - 500 095
☎ 040-24737290
✉ vspublishershyd@gmail.com

Follow us on:   

BUY OUR BOOKS FROM: AMAZON FLIPKART

© **Copyright:** *V&S* PUBLISHERS
ISBN 978-81-978021-9-5
New Edition

DISCLAIMER

PUBLISHER'S NOTE

V&S Publishers has carved a significant niche in the publishing industry over the last decade, having successfully published more than 1000 titles across 9 languages spanning over 50 subject categories. Being known for the quality of content, we have built a reputation of excellence and reliability. We have consistently delivered **"Value & Substance"** to our readers, through a wide range of titles across a variety of genres covering school books, fiction and non-fiction that caters to different people from every section of the society.

The **Olympiad Guidebooks for classes 1-10** across all subjects, launched almost a decade ago, under the **GEN X Imprint**, became a go-to-source for the school students in no time, owing to their invaluable and substantive content written in a guidebook pattern,.

Having successfully sold a million copies of the same and in response to demand by both students as well as shopkeepers nationwide; we now present before you our newly launched **Olympiad Workbook Series**, designed for **classes 1-10 across 4 subjects**.

The workbooks are meticulously curated by a team of experienced educators, researchers and subject matter experts, edited by professionals and peer reviewed by teachers. The team has poured its efforts and expertise into creating a crisp and concise workbook which will help and guide the students to the path of success in Olympiad exams. The **MCQs** identified will not only help in scoring top marks in Olympiads but also inculcate a sense of deeper understanding of the subject, by way of solving **HOTS** and referring to complete solutions at the end of the book.

Here we present our new release– **OLYMPIAD WORKBOOK (IEO) CLASS–2** having following features:

- ☞ Based on the latest syllabi
- ☞ MCQs with comprehensive coverage of topics
- ☞ HOTS Questions liberally included
- ☞ A dedicated chapter on logical reasoning
- ☞ Model test paper for thorough practice
- ☞ Sample OMR sheet for real time simulation

We have made sure through our best efforts, that this workbook strictly follows the latest syllabi and patterns of the Olympiad Examination.

As **V&S Publishers** continuously strive to enhance the readability and maintain the credibility of our academic publications, we seek the support of our valuable readers in influencing and enriching the lives of future generations of students.

P.S. While every care has been taken to ensure the correctness of the content, if you come across any error, howsoever minor, do not hesitate to discuss with teachers while pointing that out to us in no uncertain terms.

We wish you all the best for your exams!

DISTINCTIVE FEATURES

01

Learning Objectives

They list the whole chapter as subtopics, helping the teachers to guide children in a step-by-step manner.

02

Multiple Choice Questions

MCQs act as an excellent learning aid, helping you to understand and work on your mistakes.

03

HOTS (Achievers Section)

The High Order Thinking Questions aim to help the student to solve Application-based questions and gain practical understanding of the subject.

Model Test Paper

Model test paper are provided at the end of each book, which help the student to test the knowledge which they have gained after thorough reading of all chapters.

04

Answer Key

Detailed Answer Key along with explanations aid the pupil to indentify, understand the mistakes they make during the course of Olympiad preparation.

05

CONTENTS

PICTURE QUIZ

LEARNING OBJECTIVES

➤ Identifying the picture
➤ Identifying term related to picture

PRACTICE EXERCISE

1. Identify the picture
   (A) Whale
   (B) Crab
   (C) Octopus
   (D) Snail

2. Identify the picture
   (A) Lizard
   (B) Squirrel
   (C) Chameleon
   (D) Snake

3. Identify the picture
   (A) Bee
   (B) Butterfly
   (C) Cockroach
   (D) Beetle

4. Identify the picture
   (A) Deer
   (B) Chimpanzee
   (C) Monkey
   (D) Bear

5. Identify the picture
   (A) Crocodile
   (B) Dolphin
   (C) Shark
   (D) Sea horse

6. Identify the picture
   (A) Hen
   (B) Crow
   (C) Parrot
   (D) Owl

7. Identify the picture
   (A) Donkey
   (B) Horse
   (C) Zebra
   (D) Giraffe

8. Identify the picture
   (A) Cat
   (B) Lion
   (C) Dog
   (D) Mouse

9. Identify the picture
   (A) Hippopotamus
   (B) Crocodile
   (C) Alligator
   (D) Rhinoceros

10. Identify the picture
    (A) Sweater
    (B) Shirt
    (C) Top
    (D) Coat

11. Identify the picture
    (A) Ribbon
    (B) Hair band
    (C) Hair clip
    (D) Comb

12. Identify the picture
    (A) Wallet
    (B) Clutch purse
    (C) Handbag
    (D) School bag

13. Identify the picture
    (A) Shoes
    (B) Hat
    (C) Cap
    (D) Socks

14. Identify the picture
    (A) Museum
    (B) Stadium
    (C) Church
    (D) Townhouse

15. Identify the picture
    (A) Table
    (B) Chest of drawers
    (C) Refrigerator
    (D) Cupboard

16. Identify the picture
    (A) Water bottle
    (B) Lamp
    (C) Flower vase
    (D) Clock

17. Identify the picture
    (A) Swing
    (B) Table
    (C) Sofa
    (D) Chair

18. Identify the body parts
    (A) Teeth
    (B) Tongue
    (C) Eyebrow
    (D) Lips

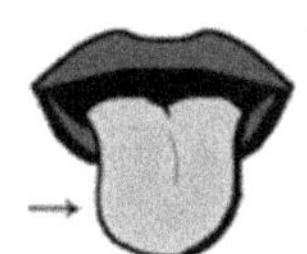

19. Identify the body parts
    (A) Face
    (B) Mole
    (C) Nose
    (D) Eye

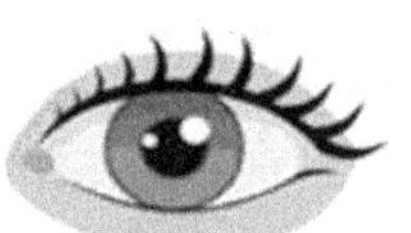

20. Identify the body parts
    (A) Thumb
    (B) Fingers
    (C) Nails
    (D) Wrist

HOTS (ACHIEVERS SECTION)

21. Identify the collective noun that relates to the picture:
    (A) Set of cushions
    (B) Set of bowls
    (C) Set of cups
    (D) Set of shoes

22. Identify the collective noun that relates to the picture:
    (A) Set of false teeth
    (B) Set of rules
    (C) Set of novels
    (D) Set of chairs

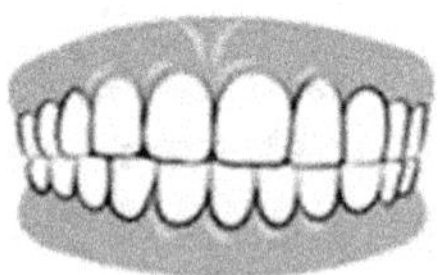

23. Dentify the collective noun that relates to the picture:
    (A) String of beads
    (B) String of pebbles
    (C) String of peas
    (D) String of flowers

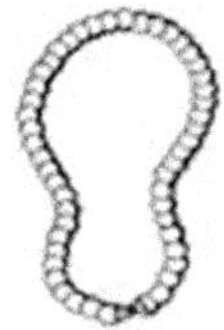

24. Identify the collective noun that relates to the picture:
    (A) A pair of slippers
    (B) A pair of jeans
    (C) A pair of glasses
    (D) A pair of scissors

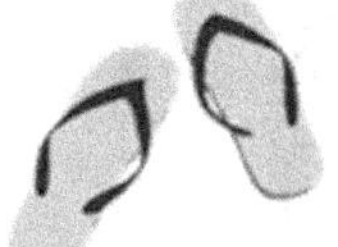

———Darken Your Choice with HB Pencil———

1.	A B C D	6.	A B C D	11.	A B C D	16	A B C D	21.	A B C D
2.	A B C D	7.	A B C D	12.	A B C D	17.	A B C D	22.	A B C D
3.	A B C D	8.	A B C D	13.	A B C D	18.	A B C D	23.	A B C D
4.	A B C D	9.	A B C D	14.	A B C D	19.	A B C D	24.	A B C D
5.	A B C D	10.	A B C D	15.	A B C D	20.	A B C D		

A WORLD OF WORDS

LEARNING OBJECTIVES

➤ Animals and their types
➤ Household items

➤ Different emotions

PRACTICE EXERCISE

I. Choose the correct animal for the following sounds.

1. Bark
   - (A) Duck
   - (B) Stallion
   - (C) Dog
   - (D) Fox

2. Cackle
   - (A) Owl
   - (B) Pigs
   - (C) Bull
   - (D) Rooster

3. Grunt
   - (A) Hen
   - (B) Camel
   - (C) Cow
   - (D) Mouse

4. Buzz
   - (A) Rabbit
   - (B) Bee
   - (C) Camel
   - (D) Dog

5. Chatter
   - (A) Monkey
   - (B) Lion
   - (C) Owl
   - (D) Jackal

II. Choose the correct option:

6. All human beings need the following:
   - (A) Food
   - (B) Clothes
   - (C) Shelter
   - (D) All of these

7. Mainly, food is obtained from the following:
   - (A) Plants
   - (B) Animals
   - (C) Both
   - (D) None of these

8. Energy to do any work can obtained from the following:
   - (A) Food
   - (B) House
   - (C) Clothes
   - (D) All of these

9. We obtain the medicines from the following plants such as–
   - (A) Tulsi
   - (B) Neem
   - (C) Cincona
   - (D) All of these

OLYMPIAD WORKBOOK (IEO) CLASS– 2

10. Which of them is odd in the following?
   (A) Groundnut
   (B) Mustard
   (C) Fruits
   (D) Coconut
11. Which of the following is not obtained from plants?
   (A) Spices
   (B) Medicines
   (C) Eggs
   (D) Pulses
12. Meat can be obtained from the following?
   (A) Goat
   (B) Hen
   (C) Fish
   (D) All of these
13. Which of the food items provide us energy:
   (A) Sugar
   (B) Glucose
   (C) Wheat
   (D) All of these
14. Shreya: Protein helps is to grow stronger.

   Ananya: Green vegetables helps us to prevent diseases and remain healthy.
   (A) Shreya is wrong and Ananya is right
   (B) Both Shreya and Ananya are right
   (C) Both Shreya and Ananya are wrong
   (D) None of these
15. Many food items can be eaten in different way(s). Such as
   (A) Raw
   (B) Cooked
   (C) Both
   (D) None of these

III. How would you feel in the following situations?

16. When you get to see a movie, you really like. _______________________
17. When you are looking forward to eating ice cream but your mother refuses. _______________________
18. When you open your present and realize that your younger brother has broken it already. _______________________
19. When your father finds out that you have broken his favourite pen. _______________________
20. When your friend tells you a scary story. _______________________
21. When you realize that your mother will not be able to make your favourite dish as she is unwell._______________________
22. When you try to ride a bicycle again and again but are not able to. _______________________
23. When you don't know if you should eat the chocolate that the guest is offering. You don't know if Mum will approve or not. _______________________
24. When Dad gifts you play station. _______________________
25. When you think mother is going to scold you but she doesn't. _______________________
26. When Grandmother forces you to eat bitter gourd which you hate . _______________________
27. When it's your cousin's wedding and no one lets you sleep. _______________________
28. When there is no electricity and no one to play with so you have to stay at home with nothing to do. _______________________
29. When your neighbour pulls your cheeks and laughs when you are in pain. _______________________
30. When mother finds out that you finished all the sweets without telling anyone. _______________________

IV. What kind of animals live in these homes?

31. Burrow   : __________
32. Pen   : __________
33. Cave   : __________
34. Den   : __________
35. Anthill   : __________

V. Identify the meal to which the given food items belong.

36. Poha   : __________
37. Dosa   : __________

38. Samosa   : __________
39. Cookies   : __________
40. Coffee   : __________

VI. Choose the correct emotion for the following:

41. Hate   : __________
42. Compassion : __________
43. Despair   : __________
44. Bliss   : __________
45. Anxiety   : __________

⏰ ⏰ ⏰

——— Darken Your Choice with HB Pencil ———

1. Ⓐ Ⓑ Ⓒ Ⓓ	10. Ⓐ Ⓑ Ⓒ Ⓓ	19. Ⓐ Ⓑ Ⓒ Ⓓ	28 Ⓐ Ⓑ Ⓒ Ⓓ	37. Ⓐ Ⓑ Ⓒ Ⓓ
2. Ⓐ Ⓑ Ⓒ Ⓓ	11. Ⓐ Ⓑ Ⓒ Ⓓ	20. Ⓐ Ⓑ Ⓒ Ⓓ	29. Ⓐ Ⓑ Ⓒ Ⓓ	38. Ⓐ Ⓑ Ⓒ Ⓓ
3. Ⓐ Ⓑ Ⓒ Ⓓ	12. Ⓐ Ⓑ Ⓒ Ⓓ	21. Ⓐ Ⓑ Ⓒ Ⓓ	30. Ⓐ Ⓑ Ⓒ Ⓓ	39. Ⓐ Ⓑ Ⓒ Ⓓ
4. Ⓐ Ⓑ Ⓒ Ⓓ	13. Ⓐ Ⓑ Ⓒ Ⓓ	22. Ⓐ Ⓑ Ⓒ Ⓓ	31. Ⓐ Ⓑ Ⓒ Ⓓ	40. Ⓐ Ⓑ Ⓒ Ⓓ
5. Ⓐ Ⓑ Ⓒ Ⓓ	14. Ⓐ Ⓑ Ⓒ Ⓓ	23. Ⓐ Ⓑ Ⓒ Ⓓ	32. Ⓐ Ⓑ Ⓒ Ⓓ	41. Ⓐ Ⓑ Ⓒ Ⓓ
6. Ⓐ Ⓑ Ⓒ Ⓓ	15. Ⓐ Ⓑ Ⓒ Ⓓ	24. Ⓐ Ⓑ Ⓒ Ⓓ	33. Ⓐ Ⓑ Ⓒ Ⓓ	42. Ⓐ Ⓑ Ⓒ Ⓓ
7. Ⓐ Ⓑ Ⓒ Ⓓ	16. Ⓐ Ⓑ Ⓒ Ⓓ	25. Ⓐ Ⓑ Ⓒ Ⓓ	34. Ⓐ Ⓑ Ⓒ Ⓓ	43. Ⓐ Ⓑ Ⓒ Ⓓ
8. Ⓐ Ⓑ Ⓒ Ⓓ	17. Ⓐ Ⓑ Ⓒ Ⓓ	26. Ⓐ Ⓑ Ⓒ Ⓓ	35. Ⓐ Ⓑ Ⓒ Ⓓ	44. Ⓐ Ⓑ Ⓒ Ⓓ
9. Ⓐ Ⓑ Ⓒ Ⓓ	18. Ⓐ Ⓑ Ⓒ Ⓓ	27. Ⓐ Ⓑ Ⓒ Ⓓ	36. Ⓐ Ⓑ Ⓒ Ⓓ	45. Ⓐ Ⓑ Ⓒ Ⓓ

WORD POWER : SYNONYMS AND ANTONYMS

➤ Usage of words in different way

PRACTICE EXERCISE

I. Choose the word that best expresses the meaning of the word given in capital letters.

1. BRIEF
   - (A) Limited
   - (B) Small
   - (C) Little
   - (D) Short

2. ALERT
   - (A) Energetic
   - (B) Observant
   - (C) Intelligent
   - (D) Watchful

3. WARRIOR
   - (A) Soldier
   - (B) Sailor
   - (C) Pirate
   - (D) Spy

4. DISTANT
   - (A) Far
   - (B) Removed
   - (C) Reserved
   - (D) Separate

5. FAKE
   - (A) Original
   - (B) Imitation
   - (C) Trustworthy
   - (D) Loyal

6. ATTEMPT
   - (A) Serve
   - (B) Explore
   - (C) Try
   - (D) Explain

II. Choose the word that is almost opposite in meaning to the word given in capital letters.

7. CONTAIN
   - (A) Exclude
   - (B) Accept
   - (C) Unite
   - (D) Remove

8. COMMON
   - (A) Standard
   - (B) Unusual
   - (C) Scary
   - (D) Super

9. SCHEDULED
   - (A) Assigned
   - (B) Prepared
   - (C) Unplanned
   - (D) Late

10. CLEVER
    - (A) Splendid
    - (B) Smart
    - (C) Sassy
    - (D) Stupid

11. ATTRACT
    - (A) Depend
    - (B) Delight
    - (C) Disgust
    - (D) Disable

12. CONSIDER
    - (A) Think
    - (B) Ignore
    - (C) Finish
    - (D) Study

III. Fill in the blanks with the correct options.

13. Can I go to the store, _____ ?
    - (A) too
    - (B) to
    - (C) two
    - (D) None of the above

14. The number _____ comes before the number three.
    - (A) too
    - (B) to
    - (C) two
    - (D) tow

15. I think I _____ my mother calling.
    - (A) hear
    - (B) here
    - (C) hair
    - (D) None of the above

Read the poem given below and answer the questions from the options given below.

I am a brat I love to laugh, though it is tough When you (16)____, I love to play When you want me study whole (17) ____, I want to cry For games you don't even (18) ____. I love to laugh at the clown When you all (19) ____ do you know What? It's not easy to be a (20) ____.

16. The rhyming word for laugh here would be
    (A) Calf
    (B) Half
    (C) Cough
    (D) Walf

17. The rhyming word for play here would be
    (A) Day
    (B) May
    (C) Say
    (D) Stay

18. The rhyming word for cry here would be
    (A) Fry
    (B) Try
    (C) Dry
    (D) My

19. The rhyming word for clown would be
    (A) Down
    (B) Frown
    (C) Mown
    (D) Brown

20. The rhyming word for what here is:
    (A) Brat
    (B) Cat
    (C) Mat
    (D) Rat

—Darken Your Choice with HB Pencil—

1.	Ⓐ Ⓑ Ⓒ Ⓓ	5.	Ⓐ Ⓑ Ⓒ Ⓓ	9.	Ⓐ Ⓑ Ⓒ Ⓓ	13	Ⓐ Ⓑ Ⓒ Ⓓ	17.	Ⓐ Ⓑ Ⓒ Ⓓ
2.	Ⓐ Ⓑ Ⓒ Ⓓ	6.	Ⓐ Ⓑ Ⓒ Ⓓ	10.	Ⓐ Ⓑ Ⓒ Ⓓ	14.	Ⓐ Ⓑ Ⓒ Ⓓ	18.	Ⓐ Ⓑ Ⓒ Ⓓ
3.	Ⓐ Ⓑ Ⓒ Ⓓ	7.	Ⓐ Ⓑ Ⓒ Ⓓ	11.	Ⓐ Ⓑ Ⓒ Ⓓ	15.	Ⓐ Ⓑ Ⓒ Ⓓ	19.	Ⓐ Ⓑ Ⓒ Ⓓ
4.	Ⓐ Ⓑ Ⓒ Ⓓ	8.	Ⓐ Ⓑ Ⓒ Ⓓ	12.	Ⓐ Ⓑ Ⓒ Ⓓ	16.	Ⓐ Ⓑ Ⓒ Ⓓ	20.	Ⓐ Ⓑ Ⓒ Ⓓ

NOUNS

LEARNING OBJECTIVES

➤ Nouns and its different types

PRACTICE EXERCISE

I. **Select the correct option that identifies the noun in the sentence.**

1. Winter is very cold.
   - (A) Winter
   - (B) Very
   - (C) Cold
   - (D) None of the above

2. The man was tall.
   - (A) The
   - (B) Man
   - (C) Was
   - (D) None of the above

3. Close the gate.
   - (A) Close
   - (B) The
   - (C) Gate
   - (D) None of the above

4. The car moved fast.
   - (A) Car
   - (B) Moved
   - (C) Fast
   - (D) None of the above

5. School started early.
   - (A) School
   - (B) Started
   - (C) Early
   - (D) None of the above

6. Catch the ball.
   - (A) Catch
   - (B) The
   - (C) Ball
   - (D) None of the above

7. The doctor worked fast.
   - (A) The
   - (B) Doctor
   - (C) Fast
   - (D) None of the above

8. Open the door.
   - (A) The
   - (B) Door
   - (C) Open
   - (D) None of the above

9. The girl was happy.
   - (A) Was
   - (B) The
   - (C) Girl
   - (D) None of the above

10. Look at the moon.
    - (A) Look
    - (B) At
    - (C) Moon
    - (D) None of the above

II. Choose the correct common noun in every sentence from the options given below.

11. Mr. Davis loves to eat pizza.
    (A) Mr. Davis   (B) loves
    (C) eat   (D) pizza

12. Kelly goes to Dunbar Elementary school.
    (A) Kelly
    (B) Dunbar Elementary
    (C) School
    (D) None of the above

III. Choose the correct form of the noun and fill in the blanks.

13. I have three ______________.
    (A) child   (B) children
    (C) childs   (D) none of these

14. There are five ______________ and one ______________.
    (A) man, woman   (B) men, woman
    (C) man, women   (D) none of these

15. __________ play with bottles as toys.
    (A) Baby   (B) Babies
    (C) Babes   (D) none of these

16. I put two big __________ in the lunch box.
    (A) potatoes   (B) potato
    (C) potatos   (D) none of these

17. Some men wear __________.
    (A) watches   (B) watch
    (C) watchs   (D) none of these

18. I put a ________ on the desk.
    (A) memo   (B) memos
    (C) momos   (D) none of these

19. I saw a __________ running by.
    (A) mose   (B) mice
    (C) mouse   (D) none of these

20. There are few __________ on the road today.
    (A) bus   (B) buses
    (C) busses   (D) none of these

21. The cat is sitting on my __________.
    (A) bed   (B) bedding
    (C) beds   (D) none of these

22. There are five __________ on my desk.
    (A) pencils   (B) pencil
    (C) pencilss   (D) none of these

IV. Choose the correct feminine gender of the underlined word.

23. I saw a <u>deer</u> in the zoo.
    (A) sow   (B) hen
    (C) doe   (D) none of these

24. The <u>peacock</u> was dancing.
    (A) mare   (B) duck
    (C) peahen   (D) none of these

25. John was riding a <u>horse</u>.
    (A) mare   (B) queen
    (C) sow   (D) none of these

26. A <u>lion</u> eats the flesh of other animals.
    (A) peahen   (B) cow
    (C) lioness   (D) none of these

27. The <u>pig</u> is a very filthy animal.
    (A) doe   (B) sow
    (C) queen   (D) none of these

28. Human beings eat the flesh of <u>cock</u>.
    (A) hen   (B) bitch
    (C) mare   (D) none of these

29. I saw a group of <u>drakes</u> in the lake.
    (A) duck   (B) cow
    (C) hen   (D) none of these

30. A <u>cat</u> can climb up a tree.
    (A) queen   (B) bitch
    (C) duck   (D) none of these

Fill with appropriate noun:

31. Give me a __________ and some __________ to write a letter.
    - (A) pencils, book
    - (B) pen, paper
    - (C) table, chair
    - (D) chalk, blackboard

32. There is an __________ and a __________ on the branch.
    - (A) bird, nest
    - (B) owl, crow
    - (C) fruit, flower
    - (D) buds, leaf

33. I listened to __________ and sang two __________.
    - (A) music, song
    - (B) music, songs
    - (C) musics, songs
    - (D) muscis, song

34. I had __________ and an __________ for my breakfast.
    - (A) apple, banana
    - (B) milk, bread
    - (C) milk, apple
    - (D) bread, banana

35. There are many __________ in this __________.
    - (A) wolfs, forests
    - (B) wolf, forests
    - (C) wolves, forest
    - (D) wolfs, forest

—Darken Your Choice with HB Pencil—

	A B C D		A B C D		A B C D		A B C D		A B C D
1.	Ⓐ Ⓑ Ⓒ Ⓓ	8.	Ⓐ Ⓑ Ⓒ Ⓓ	15.	Ⓐ Ⓑ Ⓒ Ⓓ	22	Ⓐ Ⓑ Ⓒ Ⓓ	29.	Ⓐ Ⓑ Ⓒ Ⓓ
2.	Ⓐ Ⓑ Ⓒ Ⓓ	9.	Ⓐ Ⓑ Ⓒ Ⓓ	16.	Ⓐ Ⓑ Ⓒ Ⓓ	23.	Ⓐ Ⓑ Ⓒ Ⓓ	30.	Ⓐ Ⓑ Ⓒ Ⓓ
3.	Ⓐ Ⓑ Ⓒ Ⓓ	10.	Ⓐ Ⓑ Ⓒ Ⓓ	17.	Ⓐ Ⓑ Ⓒ Ⓓ	24.	Ⓐ Ⓑ Ⓒ Ⓓ	31.	Ⓐ Ⓑ Ⓒ Ⓓ
4.	Ⓐ Ⓑ Ⓒ Ⓓ	11.	Ⓐ Ⓑ Ⓒ Ⓓ	18.	Ⓐ Ⓑ Ⓒ Ⓓ	25.	Ⓐ Ⓑ Ⓒ Ⓓ	32.	Ⓐ Ⓑ Ⓒ Ⓓ
5.	Ⓐ Ⓑ Ⓒ Ⓓ	12.	Ⓐ Ⓑ Ⓒ Ⓓ	19.	Ⓐ Ⓑ Ⓒ Ⓓ	26.	Ⓐ Ⓑ Ⓒ Ⓓ	33.	Ⓐ Ⓑ Ⓒ Ⓓ
6.	Ⓐ Ⓑ Ⓒ Ⓓ	13.	Ⓐ Ⓑ Ⓒ Ⓓ	20.	Ⓐ Ⓑ Ⓒ Ⓓ	27.	Ⓐ Ⓑ Ⓒ Ⓓ	34.	Ⓐ Ⓑ Ⓒ Ⓓ
7.	Ⓐ Ⓑ Ⓒ Ⓓ	14.	Ⓐ Ⓑ Ⓒ Ⓓ	21.	Ⓐ Ⓑ Ⓒ Ⓓ	28.	Ⓐ Ⓑ Ⓒ Ⓓ	35.	Ⓐ Ⓑ Ⓒ Ⓓ

PRONOUNS

LEARNING OBJECTIVES

➤ Pronouns and its different types

PRACTICE EXERCISE

I. Choose the type of pronoun the underlined word is.

1. <u>Which</u> of these books is yours, Aditi?
   (A) Reflexive   (B) Demonstrative
   (C) Interrogative   (D) Relative

2. Everyone in the group should shake hands with <u>one another</u>.
   (A) Relative   (B) Reciprocal
   (C) Demonstrative   (D) Interrogative

3. When I asked her about it, she told me it was <u>her</u> bag that was stolen.
   (A) Possessive   (B) Interrogative
   (C) Reflexive   (D) Relative

4. Those <u>who</u> wish to see the Taj can come with me.
   (A) Interrogative   (B) Demonstrative
   (C) Relative   (D) Reflexive

5. Since it was a buffet, he started helping <u>himself</u> to the food.
   (A) Demonstrative   (B) Reflexive
   (C) Relative   (D) Interrogative

6. <u>These</u> are the songs which Alisha likes.
   (A) Relative   (B) Demonstrative
   (C) Interrogative   (D) Reflexive

7. Sharad told me that <u>his</u> playstation was not working anymore.
   (A) Interrogative   (B) Reflexive
   (C) Demonstrative   (D) Possessive

8. When I asked them the question, they merely looked at <u>each other</u>.
   (A) Reciprocal   (B) Interrogative
   (C) Demonstrative   (D) Reflexive

9. <u>Which</u> of these places do you want to go to?
   (A) Possessive   (B) Interrogative
   (C) Demonstrative   (D) Reflexive

10. Don't worry so much, <u>someone</u> from the telephone company will definitely come today and repair your connection.
    (A) Reflexive   (B) Possessive
    (C) Indefinite   (D) Demonstrative

11. Take <u>this</u> candle and place it in the other room.
    (A) Possessive   (B) Reflexive
    (C) Reciprocal   (D) Demonstrative

12. <u>Everyone</u> wears new clothes on Diwali.
    (A) Indefinite   (B) Possessive
    (C) Demonstrative (D) Reciprocal

13. <u>Which</u> of the movies do you want to see today?
    (A) Demonstrative (B) Interrogative
    (C) Reflexive   (D) Possessive

14. When I asked him to give me the directions, he was <u>himself</u> confused.
    (A) Reflexive   (B) Demonstrative

OLYMPIAD WORKBOOK (IEO) CLASS— 2

(C) Possessive   (D) Reciprocal

15. <u>Someone</u> had forgotten to switch off the lights.
   (A) Possessive
   (B) Demonstrative
   (C) Indefinite
   (D) Reciprocal

II. Choose the correct pronoun to complete the sentence.

16. Sakshi was looking for __________ who has a blue sweater.
   (A) Herself   (B) It
   (C) There   (D) Someone

17. Arun voted for __________ in the class elections.
   (A) Himself   (B) Where
   (C) Each other   (D) Their

18. __________ pet dog was not feeling very well today. She was very upset.
   (A) It   (B) Her
   (C) Everyone   (D) One another

19. Ravi is a successful doctor __________ lives in Delhi.
   (A) It   (B) His
   (C) Who   (D) Anyone

20. Can __________ tell me what the story of this movie is?
   (A) Hers   (B) Anyone
   (C) Them   (D) Which

21. The car __________ was supposed to pick me up was already late.
   (A) No one   (B) It
   (C) Which   (D) He

22. Renu is a great painter. __________ is one of her paintings.
   (A) Which   (B) Whom
   (C) Any   (D) This

23. Where is that shop __________ is famous for its street food?
   (A) Their   (B) Which
   (C) It   (D) Nobody

24. Neha exclaimed, "__________ is my bag!"
   (A) No one   (B) Whom
   (C) Her   (D) That

25. Amit looked at __________ car and said that he wanted to buy a new one.
   (A) What   (B) He
   (C) His   (D) Each other

26. He said, "I can't go out in __________ state! Let me change."
   (A) It   (B) This
   (C) Who   (D) His

27. __________ is our president and we support him fully.
   (A) He
   (B) It
   (C) Someone
   (D) Their

28. She picked up a colourful scarf as a gift for __________.
   (A) Someone
   (B) It
   (C) Their
   (D) Herself

29. This is the newest phone and __________ is amazing!
   (A) Someone
   (B) It
   (C) No one
   (D) He

30. __________ are coming to visit and will stay for a week.
   (A) It   (B) Oneself
   (C) They   (D) Who

Identify the kind of pronouns that are underlined in the following sentences.

31. Give the students <u>their</u> notebooks.

32. I have <u>myself</u> seen the parade.

33. <u>Someone</u> should open the door.

34. Give this to the girl <u>who</u> was sitting here.

35. I will buy <u>that</u> pen in the shelf.

—Darken Your Choice with HB Pencil—

1. Ⓐ Ⓑ Ⓒ Ⓓ	8. Ⓐ Ⓑ Ⓒ Ⓓ	15. Ⓐ Ⓑ Ⓒ Ⓓ	22 Ⓐ Ⓑ Ⓒ Ⓓ	29. Ⓐ Ⓑ Ⓒ Ⓓ
2. Ⓐ Ⓑ Ⓒ Ⓓ	9. Ⓐ Ⓑ Ⓒ Ⓓ	16. Ⓐ Ⓑ Ⓒ Ⓓ	23. Ⓐ Ⓑ Ⓒ Ⓓ	30. Ⓐ Ⓑ Ⓒ Ⓓ
3. Ⓐ Ⓑ Ⓒ Ⓓ	10. Ⓐ Ⓑ Ⓒ Ⓓ	17. Ⓐ Ⓑ Ⓒ Ⓓ	24. Ⓐ Ⓑ Ⓒ Ⓓ	31. Ⓐ Ⓑ Ⓒ Ⓓ
4. Ⓐ Ⓑ Ⓒ Ⓓ	11. Ⓐ Ⓑ Ⓒ Ⓓ	18. Ⓐ Ⓑ Ⓒ Ⓓ	25. Ⓐ Ⓑ Ⓒ Ⓓ	32. Ⓐ Ⓑ Ⓒ Ⓓ
5. Ⓐ Ⓑ Ⓒ Ⓓ	12. Ⓐ Ⓑ Ⓒ Ⓓ	19. Ⓐ Ⓑ Ⓒ Ⓓ	26. Ⓐ Ⓑ Ⓒ Ⓓ	33. Ⓐ Ⓑ Ⓒ Ⓓ
6. Ⓐ Ⓑ Ⓒ Ⓓ	13. Ⓐ Ⓑ Ⓒ Ⓓ	20. Ⓐ Ⓑ Ⓒ Ⓓ	27. Ⓐ Ⓑ Ⓒ Ⓓ	34. Ⓐ Ⓑ Ⓒ Ⓓ
7. Ⓐ Ⓑ Ⓒ Ⓓ	14. Ⓐ Ⓑ Ⓒ Ⓓ	21. Ⓐ Ⓑ Ⓒ Ⓓ	28. Ⓐ Ⓑ Ⓒ Ⓓ	35. Ⓐ Ⓑ Ⓒ Ⓓ

VERBS

LEARNING OBJECTIVES

➤ Verbs and its different types

➤ Modal verbs

PRACTICE EXERCISE

I. Choose the correct options to fill in the blanks.

1. I am not sure what to _______ today evening.
    - (A) Wore
    - (B) Wear
    - (C) Is wearing
    - (D) Has weared

2. Last evening, we were all standing on the roof of a tall building when a plane _______ past us!
    - (A) Fly
    - (B) Flew
    - (C) Flying
    - (D) Flied

3. Can you please _______ an email to Sarah telling her about our plan?
    - (A) Write
    - (B) Wrote
    - (C) Written
    - (D) Right

4. Amit _______ a lot of money last month on his Europe vacation.
    - (A) Spend
    - (B) Spended
    - (C) Spent
    - (D) Has spend

5. Natasha assured me that she will _______ the uniforms today.
    - (A) Send
    - (B) Sent
    - (C) Has spend
    - (D) Has spent

6. Aditya had already _______ by the time we reached last night.
    - (A) Leave
    - (B) Leaved
    - (C) Left
    - (D) Be leaving

7. I am a big fan of this game. I will _______ it on the day it releases!
    - (A) Bought
    - (B) Buyer
    - (C) Has Bought
    - (D) Buy

8. The accountant _______ irritated last time because we did not have all the papers.
    - (A) Get
    - (B) Gets
    - (C) Got
    - (D) Gotten

9. My mother had _______ me about the event last night but I forgot.
    - (A) Told
    - (B) Tell
    - (C) Telling
    - (D) Is Telling

10. They always _______ to the station half an hour before the train reaches.
    - (A) Will come
    - (B) Come
    - (C) Came
    - (D) Comes

II. Choose the correct options to fill in the blanks.

11. I _______ see you tomorrow.
    - (A) Will
    - (B) Going go
    - (C) Am
    - (D) Do

12. She _______ finished lunch by the time he arrived.
    - (A) Has
    - (B) Had
    - (C) Was
    - (D) Did

13. What time ___ he usually get up?
    (A) Do   (B) Does
    (C) Is   (D) Has
14. They ____ getting ready when she arrived.
    (A) Did   (B) Have
    (C) Were   (D) Do
15. I _____ usually make so many mistakes.
    (A) Didn't   (B) Don't
    (C) Hadn't   (D) Wouldn't

III. Fill in the blanks with the correct 'Modal Verb' from the options provided.

16. I know only my mother tongue, Hindi. __________
    (A) I can speak Tamil.
    (B) I cannot understand Hindi.
    (C) I can speak Hindi.
    (D) I can speak Bengali.

17. Meena is studying in class II. She is very tired. Can she stay awake the whole night? __________
    (A) Yes, she can.
    (B) Yes, she can't.
    (C) No, she can't.
    (D) No, I can't.

18. I know numbers only up to 100. _________
    (A) I can count up to 1000.
    (B) I can count only up to 100.
    (C) I can write up to 1000.
    (D) I can write numbers after 100.

19. I have learnt how to ride a bicycle. __________
    (A) I can drive a car.
    (B) I can ride a bicycle.
    (C) Can you teach me to ride a bicycle?
    (D) I cannot ride a bicycle.

20. It is only 8 o'clock. _______________
    (A) I cannot reach the place.
    (B) I can be there in time.
    (C) Can you tell me what the time is?
    (D) Can you lend me your watch?

21. I find it difficult to ride a horse. ___What should I do?
    (A) Can you ride a horse?
    (B) I can ride a horse even at night.
    (C) I can't ride a horse well.
    (D) I will teach you how to ride a horse easily.

22. We have a guitar lying idle at home. _________
    (A) My brother plays it.
    (B) I can't play it.
    (C) My father plays it.
    (D) My sister plays the guitar.

23. My brother has learnt the alphabet till M. _________
    (A) He can point out S.
    (B) He can point out Z.
    (C) He can recognize B.
    (D) He can write in cursive.

24. We have a shop nearby, but I don't buy anything. ________
    (A) We can buy many things there.
    (B) I can't count money.
    (C) Can we buy there?
    (D) No one can buy anything there.

25. Sanskrit is not being taught to us in the class. _________
    (A) So, I can write poems in Sanskrit.
    (B) So, I cannot understand Sanskrit but can write in Sanskrit.
    (C) So, I cannot speak Sanskrit.
    (D) So, we can learn Sanskrit now in the class.

OLYMPIAD WORKBOOK (IEO) CLASS – 2

Choose the correct modal for the following situations:

26. ________________ you have a long life!

27. ________________ I take one more sweet?

28. Nina ________________ come tomorrow. She definitely seemed interested.

29. ________________ you like some biscuits with your tea?

30. You ________________ never talk while eating.

1.	Ⓐ Ⓑ Ⓒ Ⓓ	7.	Ⓐ Ⓑ Ⓒ Ⓓ	13.	Ⓐ Ⓑ Ⓒ Ⓓ	19	Ⓐ Ⓑ Ⓒ Ⓓ	25.	Ⓐ Ⓑ Ⓒ Ⓓ
2.	Ⓐ Ⓑ Ⓒ Ⓓ	8.	Ⓐ Ⓑ Ⓒ Ⓓ	14.	Ⓐ Ⓑ Ⓒ Ⓓ	20.	Ⓐ Ⓑ Ⓒ Ⓓ	26.	Ⓐ Ⓑ Ⓒ Ⓓ
3.	Ⓐ Ⓑ Ⓒ Ⓓ	9.	Ⓐ Ⓑ Ⓒ Ⓓ	15.	Ⓐ Ⓑ Ⓒ Ⓓ	21.	Ⓐ Ⓑ Ⓒ Ⓓ	27.	Ⓐ Ⓑ Ⓒ Ⓓ
4.	Ⓐ Ⓑ Ⓒ Ⓓ	10.	Ⓐ Ⓑ Ⓒ Ⓓ	16.	Ⓐ Ⓑ Ⓒ Ⓓ	22.	Ⓐ Ⓑ Ⓒ Ⓓ	28.	Ⓐ Ⓑ Ⓒ Ⓓ
5.	Ⓐ Ⓑ Ⓒ Ⓓ	11.	Ⓐ Ⓑ Ⓒ Ⓓ	17.	Ⓐ Ⓑ Ⓒ Ⓓ	23.	Ⓐ Ⓑ Ⓒ Ⓓ	29.	Ⓐ Ⓑ Ⓒ Ⓓ
6.	Ⓐ Ⓑ Ⓒ Ⓓ	12.	Ⓐ Ⓑ Ⓒ Ⓓ	18.	Ⓐ Ⓑ Ⓒ Ⓓ	24.	Ⓐ Ⓑ Ⓒ Ⓓ	30.	Ⓐ Ⓑ Ⓒ Ⓓ

ADVERBS

LEARNING OBJECTIVES

➤ Adverbs and its examples

PRACTICE EXERCISE

I. Choose the correct option and fill in the blanks.

1. We meet ____________Sunday to play cricket in the stadium.
   (A) Soon   (B) Every
   (C) Twice   (D) Quickly

2. Tanya comes to meet me _________.
   (A) Slowly   (B) Clumsily
   (C) Often   (D) Ago

3. It started raining, so everyone moved _______________.
   (A) Above   (B) Somewhere
   (C) Closely   (D) Inside

4. She eats _________ quickly. It is not healthy.
   (A) Often   (B) Clearly
   (C) Too   (D) Here

5. When Amit heard about the accident, he came ___________
   (A) Nearly   (B) Under
   (C) Often   (D) Immediately

6. Mother knocked on the door at 1 pm. They were ___________ sleeping.
   (A) Quietly   (B) Still
   (C) Very   (D) Too

7. We came to the function last year too. It is organized ____________.
   (A) Annually   (B) Quickly

(C) Always   (D) Slowly

8. Have you kept my watch ________? I am not able to find it.
   (A) Always   (B) Often
   (C) Somewhere   (D) Here

9. Rohit is very religious. He prays _________.
   (A) Rarely   (B) Daily
   (C) Above   (D) Quickly

10. I am not surprised that she won the scholarship. She is _______ intelligent.
    (A) Beautifully (B) Nearly
    (C) Sadly   (D) So

11. _________cross the road from the zebra crossing.
    (A) Always   (B) Here
    (C) Beside   (D) Often

12. I have been sitting near the phone all day! He hasn't called _______.
    (A) Below   (B) Often
    (C) Yet   (D) Already

13. She painted the scene _________. I am speechless!
    (A) Restlessly   (B) Beautifully
    (C) Often   (D) Here

14. My grandmother has been ill for the last three months, so we go to meet her ____________.

OLYMPIAD WORKBOOK (IEO) CLASS – 2

(A) Under   (B) Happily

(C) Often   (D) Never

15. The weather was great __________. We played in the park all day.

    (A) Yesterday   (B) Often

    (C) Intently   (D) Too

16. The class was __________ full, so we started the lecture.

    (A) Twice   (B) Above

    (C) Quietly   (D) Nearly

17. I have already watched this movie once but I don't mind watching it __________.

    (A) Inside   (B) Again

    (C) Always   (D) Soon

18. Nisha is a good dancer. She practices __________.

    (A) Really

    (B) Always

    (C) Everyday

    (D) Sometimes

19. Put the cat __________ the blanket.

    (A) Under   (B) Below

    (C) Again   (D) Yet

20. I asked her if she had visited the Red Fort __________, but she told me that this was her first visit.

(A) After   (B) Inside

(C) Before   (D) Tomorrow

II. Choose the correct answer from the alternatives given in the sentences.

21. We are busy with school today. We can come and visit you again slowly/tomorrow.

22. Shahrukh has rarely/always been my favourite hero.

23. When I heard Ashish singing, I was really/poorly impressed.

24. The teacher asked Rahul to sit down and he rarely/obediently sat down.

25. When I asked her to join me for lunch, she happily/already accepted.

26. I sometimes/much like to go for a jog in the morning.

27. When he delivered my things, I asked him to keep them on/much the table.

28. By the time Anita reached the theatre, the movie had already/rarely begun.

29. The doctor advised her to take the medicine twice/inside a day.

30. They spent the Sunday lazily/slowly watching T.V.

HOTS (ACHIEVERS SECTION)

Read the following passage and fill in the blanks from the right adverb from the options given below.

Siya was a very careless girl. She would keep her things (31) __________ and forget where she had kept them. One day her mother gave her some important papers, to keep them at a safe place. Siya was looking for a safe place in her room; (32) __________ the doorbell rang. The doorbell was ringing (33) __________. Siya kept the papers on her bed and (34) __________ ran to open the door. It was the postman, who was ringing the doorbell. She took the letter that he had got and forgot about the papers. She went to the other room and started watching T.V. After watching T.V for a long time, she went back to her room, and slept till late in the evening. In the evening, when her mom asked for the papers. She had no idea, she (35) __________ ran to her room to look for those papers but could not find them.

31.

    (A) careful   (B) caring
    (C) carelessly   (D) care

32.

    (A) slowly   (B) quickly
    (C) suddenly   (D) fast

33.

    (a) quitely   (B) slowly
    (C) growingly   (D) continuously

34.

    (A) hurriedly   (B) completely
    (C) quietly   (D) rushingly

35.

    (A) quickly
    (B) unintentionally
    (C) continuously
    (D) suddenly

1.	Ⓐ Ⓑ Ⓒ Ⓓ	8.	Ⓐ Ⓑ Ⓒ Ⓓ	15.	Ⓐ Ⓑ Ⓒ Ⓓ	22	Ⓐ Ⓑ Ⓒ Ⓓ	29.	Ⓐ Ⓑ Ⓒ Ⓓ
2.	Ⓐ Ⓑ Ⓒ Ⓓ	9.	Ⓐ Ⓑ Ⓒ Ⓓ	16.	Ⓐ Ⓑ Ⓒ Ⓓ	23.	Ⓐ Ⓑ Ⓒ Ⓓ	30.	Ⓐ Ⓑ Ⓒ Ⓓ
3.	Ⓐ Ⓑ Ⓒ Ⓓ	10.	Ⓐ Ⓑ Ⓒ Ⓓ	17.	Ⓐ Ⓑ Ⓒ Ⓓ	24.	Ⓐ Ⓑ Ⓒ Ⓓ	31.	Ⓐ Ⓑ Ⓒ Ⓓ
4.	Ⓐ Ⓑ Ⓒ Ⓓ	11.	Ⓐ Ⓑ Ⓒ Ⓓ	18.	Ⓐ Ⓑ Ⓒ Ⓓ	25.	Ⓐ Ⓑ Ⓒ Ⓓ	32.	Ⓐ Ⓑ Ⓒ Ⓓ
5.	Ⓐ Ⓑ Ⓒ Ⓓ	12.	Ⓐ Ⓑ Ⓒ Ⓓ	19.	Ⓐ Ⓑ Ⓒ Ⓓ	26.	Ⓐ Ⓑ Ⓒ Ⓓ	33.	Ⓐ Ⓑ Ⓒ Ⓓ
6.	Ⓐ Ⓑ Ⓒ Ⓓ	13.	Ⓐ Ⓑ Ⓒ Ⓓ	20.	Ⓐ Ⓑ Ⓒ Ⓓ	27.	Ⓐ Ⓑ Ⓒ Ⓓ	34.	Ⓐ Ⓑ Ⓒ Ⓓ
7.	Ⓐ Ⓑ Ⓒ Ⓓ	14.	Ⓐ Ⓑ Ⓒ Ⓓ	21.	Ⓐ Ⓑ Ⓒ Ⓓ	28.	Ⓐ Ⓑ Ⓒ Ⓓ	35.	Ⓐ Ⓑ Ⓒ Ⓓ

ARTICLES

➤ Usage of Articles

PRACTICE EXERCISE

Fill in the blanks with the article 'a', 'an', or 'the' wherever necessary. Mark (d) where no article is required.

1. I like __________ blue T-shirt better than ________ red one.
    (A) a, the   (B) an, a
    (C) the, the   (D) none of these

2. Where's __________ USB drive I lent you last week?
    (A) a   (B) an
    (C) the   (D) none of these

3. Do you still live in ________ Bristol?
    (A) a   (B) an
    (C) the   (D) none of these

4. Is your mother working in __________ old office?
    (A) a   (B) an
    (C) the   (D) none of these

5. Carol's father works as ________ electrician.
    (A) a   (B) an
    (C) the   (D) none of these

6. The tomatoes are 99 pence ________ kilo.
    (A) a   (B) an
    (C) the   (D) none of these

7. What do you usually have for breakfast?
    (A) a   (B) an
    (C) the   (D) none of these

8. Ben has ________ terrible headache.
    (A) a   (B) an
    (C) the   (D) none of these

9. After this tour, you have ________ whole afternoon free to explore the city.
    (A) a   (B) an
    (C) the   (D) none of these

10. ________ aunt
    (A) a   (B) an
    (C) the   (D) none of these

11. __________ expensive bike
    (A) a   (B) an
    (C) the   (D) none of these

12. ______ bike
    (A) a   (B) an
    (C) the   (D) none of these

13. ________ one-dollar bill
    (A) a   (B) an
    (C) the   (D) none of these

14. ________ astronaut
    (A) a   (B) an
    (C) the   (D) none of these

15. ______ European school
    (A) a   (B) an
    (C) the   (D) none of these

16. ________ comic
    (A) a   (B) an
    (C) the   (D) none of these

17. ______ apple
    (A) a   (B) an
    (C) the   (D) none of these

18. _________ older sister

   (A) a   (B) an

   (C) the   (D) none of these

19. _________ eagle

   (A) a   (B) an

   (C) the   (D) none of these

20. Complete the blanks with appropriate articles.

_________ child won the first prize in _______ baby show.

   (A) The, the

   (B) The, an

   (C) An, a

   (D) A, an

HOTS (ACHIEVERS SECTION)

Directions (Qs. 1 to 10): Read the passage carefully and fill in the blanks from the options given below

Most Intelligent Man

Once upon ____ (21) ____ time, here was a man whose name was "Most intelligent". He had kept this name on his own. He always thought that there was no one in ____ (22)____ world who could defeat him in intelligence. The story of his keeping his name 'Most intelligent' goes twenty years back. That time he was as normal as any other person, and his name was also Diwakar, until he went to ____ (23) ____ temple. There ____ (24) ____ woman had lost her slippers. She was walking barefoot, and looking for her slippers. It was very hot, and ____ (25)____ Sun was its showing its full fury. It was very tough to walk on ____ (26) ____ hot floor. That woman go really troubled, and was calling for help. Diwakar came to help her. He started looking for her slippers. But could not find them. Diwakar was ____ (27) ____ cobbler by profession, he did not waste any time and made a pair of slippers in less than ____(28)____ hour. This really impressed all ____ (29) ____ people around. And ____ (30)____ chorus voice came, "Diwakar is the most intelligent".

21.

   (A) A   (B) An

   (C) The   (D) None of these

22.

   (A) A   (B) An

   (C) The   (D) None of these

23.

   (A) A   (B) An

   (C) The   (D) None of these

24.

   (A) A   (B) An

   (C) The   (D) None of these

25.

   (A) A   (B) An

   (C) The   (D) None of these

Darken Your Choice with HB Pencil

1.	Ⓐ Ⓑ Ⓒ Ⓓ	6.	Ⓐ Ⓑ Ⓒ Ⓓ	11.	Ⓐ Ⓑ Ⓒ Ⓓ	16	Ⓐ Ⓑ Ⓒ Ⓓ	21.	Ⓐ Ⓑ Ⓒ Ⓓ
2.	Ⓐ Ⓑ Ⓒ Ⓓ	7.	Ⓐ Ⓑ Ⓒ Ⓓ	12.	Ⓐ Ⓑ Ⓒ Ⓓ	17.	Ⓐ Ⓑ Ⓒ Ⓓ	22.	Ⓐ Ⓑ Ⓒ Ⓓ
3.	Ⓐ Ⓑ Ⓒ Ⓓ	8.	Ⓐ Ⓑ Ⓒ Ⓓ	13.	Ⓐ Ⓑ Ⓒ Ⓓ	18.	Ⓐ Ⓑ Ⓒ Ⓓ	23.	Ⓐ Ⓑ Ⓒ Ⓓ
4.	Ⓐ Ⓑ Ⓒ Ⓓ	9.	Ⓐ Ⓑ Ⓒ Ⓓ	14.	Ⓐ Ⓑ Ⓒ Ⓓ	19.	Ⓐ Ⓑ Ⓒ Ⓓ	24.	Ⓐ Ⓑ Ⓒ Ⓓ
5.	Ⓐ Ⓑ Ⓒ Ⓓ	10.	Ⓐ Ⓑ Ⓒ Ⓓ	15.	Ⓐ Ⓑ Ⓒ Ⓓ	20.	Ⓐ Ⓑ Ⓒ Ⓓ	25.	Ⓐ Ⓑ Ⓒ Ⓓ

PREPOSITIONS

LEARNING OBJECTIVES

➤ Usage of prepositions

PRACTICE EXERCISE

I. See the image(s) given below and fill in the blanks with appropriate prepositions.

1. The foal is standing _________ its mother.

2. The dog is running _________ the cat.

3. Number 4 is _____________ numbers 5 and 6.

II. Look at the pictures and fill in the blanks with appropriate prepositions.

4. The ball is _____________ the box.

5. The ball is _____________ the box.

6. The ball is ______the box and the bear.

7. The ball is _____________ the box.

8. The ball is ____________ the box.

9. The ball is ____________ the box.

10. The ball is ____________ the box.

III. Directions: Read the sentences and fill in the blanks from the options given below.

11. The little girl has been hiding ___ the table.
    (A) over   (B) under
    (C) above   (D) on

12. It is so hot, the sun is almost ___ our heads.
    (A) above   (B) under
    (C) in   (D) on

13. Tim lay down ___ the grass.
    (A) in   (B) on
    (C) above   (D) over

14. I saw a rainbow ___ the sky.
    (A) in   (B) on
    (C) over   (D) above

15. Why are you so late? Its half ___seven.
    (A) past   (B) on
    (C) at   (D) in

16. My dad comes home ___six o" clock.
    (A) past   (B) at
    (C) in   (D) on

17. Always wash your hands __soap before you start eating.
    (A) at   (B) in
    (C) with   (D) on

18. The bag is _____ the sofa.
    (A) above   (B) in
    (C) on   (D) under

19. Why are you hiding _____the chair?
    (A) over   (B) under
    (C) behind   (D) on

20. Where is the ball? Is it _____ the table?
    (A) above   (B) over
    (C) on   (D) under

21. I was stuck _____ the two chairs.
    (A) among   (B) between
    (C) on   (D) below

22. Mr. Milton went to the church _____ his wife.
    (A) with   (B) behind
    (C) between   (D) beside

23. I have been to my native town, it's ___ Sweden.
    (A) in   (B) on
    (C) at   (D) with

24. I saw a monkey swinging _____ one tree to another.
    (A) on   (B) in
    (C) at   (D) from

25. The bird vanished _____ its nest.
    (A) of   (B) from
    (C) on   (D) at

26. Red roses are growing ____ those plants.
    (A) on   (B) at
    (C) in   (D) among

27. The alligator is swimming ____ water.
    (A) in   (B) on
    (C) at   (D) of

28. Can't you see a peacock, ____ the two trees.

(A) behind   (B) between

(C) from   (D) above

29. The foolish crow dropped the cheese _____ its beak.

    (A) of   (B) from

    (C) in   (D) with

30. If you don't work hard, you will lag _____ your peers.

    (A) after   (B) behind

    (C) under   (D) at

HOTS (ACHIEVERS SECTION)

Directions: Read the passage given below and fill in the blanks from the options given below.

The Thirsty Crow

Once upon a time there was a crow. It was very thirsty, so it was looking for water (31) __ here to there. But it could not find water anywhere. It went (32) __ the mountains to look for water, but the mountains were dry. It was hot summer season! It went and sat (33) __ top of that mountain to be able to locate water. (34)___There it saw a group of crocodiles playing (35) __

31.

    (a) of   (b) with

    (c) from   (d) above

32.

    (a) between   (b) above

    (c) on   (d) under

33.

    (a) in   (b) on

    (c) with   (d) at

34.

    (a) from   (b) behind

    (c) under   (d) below

35.

    (a) above   (b) at

    (c) with   (d) on

Darken Your Choice with HB Pencil

1.	Ⓐ Ⓑ Ⓒ Ⓓ	8.	Ⓐ Ⓑ Ⓒ Ⓓ	15.	Ⓐ Ⓑ Ⓒ Ⓓ	22	Ⓐ Ⓑ Ⓒ Ⓓ	29.	Ⓐ Ⓑ Ⓒ Ⓓ
2.	Ⓐ Ⓑ Ⓒ Ⓓ	9.	Ⓐ Ⓑ Ⓒ Ⓓ	16.	Ⓐ Ⓑ Ⓒ Ⓓ	23.	Ⓐ Ⓑ Ⓒ Ⓓ	30.	Ⓐ Ⓑ Ⓒ Ⓓ
3.	Ⓐ Ⓑ Ⓒ Ⓓ	10.	Ⓐ Ⓑ Ⓒ Ⓓ	17.	Ⓐ Ⓑ Ⓒ Ⓓ	24.	Ⓐ Ⓑ Ⓒ Ⓓ	31.	Ⓐ Ⓑ Ⓒ Ⓓ
4.	Ⓐ Ⓑ Ⓒ Ⓓ	11.	Ⓐ Ⓑ Ⓒ Ⓓ	18.	Ⓐ Ⓑ Ⓒ Ⓓ	25.	Ⓐ Ⓑ Ⓒ Ⓓ	32.	Ⓐ Ⓑ Ⓒ Ⓓ
5.	Ⓐ Ⓑ Ⓒ Ⓓ	12.	Ⓐ Ⓑ Ⓒ Ⓓ	19.	Ⓐ Ⓑ Ⓒ Ⓓ	26.	Ⓐ Ⓑ Ⓒ Ⓓ	33.	Ⓐ Ⓑ Ⓒ Ⓓ
6.	Ⓐ Ⓑ Ⓒ Ⓓ	13.	Ⓐ Ⓑ Ⓒ Ⓓ	20.	Ⓐ Ⓑ Ⓒ Ⓓ	27.	Ⓐ Ⓑ Ⓒ Ⓓ	34.	Ⓐ Ⓑ Ⓒ Ⓓ
7.	Ⓐ Ⓑ Ⓒ Ⓓ	14.	Ⓐ Ⓑ Ⓒ Ⓓ	21.	Ⓐ Ⓑ Ⓒ Ⓓ	28.	Ⓐ Ⓑ Ⓒ Ⓓ	35.	Ⓐ Ⓑ Ⓒ Ⓓ

CONJUNCTIONS

➤ Usage of Conjunctions

PRACTICE EXERCISE

1. Wait here _____ I get back.
   (A) as soon as   (B) until
   (C) either   (D) none of these
2. I'll visit you _____ I have time.
   (A) on   (B) whenever
   (C) either   (D) none of these
3. We'll be ready ___ the time you get back.
   (A) by   (B) before
   (C) on   (D) none of these
4. We'll leave _____ we're ready.
   (A) as soon as   (B) until
   (C) either   (D) none of these
5. I'll be glad _____ it's finished.
   (A) before   (B) until
   (C) but   (D) none of these

6. We must finish it _____ we leave.
   (A) before   (B) until
   (C) either   (D) none of these
7. I hurt myself _____ I was playing tennis.
   (A) whenever   (B) while
   (C) either   (d) none of these
8. I'll give her the message _____ she arrives.
   (A) a moment   (B) the moment
   (C) when   (D) none of these
9. I'll be ready by the time she _____.
   (A) arrives   (B) will arrive
   (C) would arrive   (D) shall arrive
10. I'll only pay you _____ you finish the work.
    (A) if   (B) unless
    (C) either   (D) neither

HOTS (ACHIEVERS SECTION)

Directions: Read the passage given below and fill in the blanks choosing the answers from the options given below.

Rahul did not like to go to school, (11) ___ he liked to play with his friends. He always tried to find an excuse to not to go to school. (12) ___ he never succeeded. One day suddenly (13) ___ getting ready for school, he said he was not well. His mother got worried (14) ___ she wanted to know what had gone wrong. She did not send Rahul to the school that day. The whole day Rahul kept on lying on the bed. His mother wanted to know the problem. (15) ___ Rahul could not explain, this really worried his mom. (16) ___ she called up the doctor to visit him. The doctor came (17) ___ saw Rahul in the evening. The doctor could not diagnose the problem. This worried Rahul's mother even more. She kept on asking Rahul about how he was feeling (18) ___ he did not say anything. At 6; 30, in the evening, suddenly Rahul got up (19) ___ said that he was feeling better (20) ___ was going out to play. The moment Rahul said that his mother realized the problem. She came to know that (21) ___ he did not want to go to school (22) ___ he made this excuse. She was very angry. That day she did not allow him to go to play (23), ___ he had lied, he had to face the punishment (24) ___ his mother decided that she would call up his dad to tell him about today's incident. Rahul was very scared, (25) ___ he apologized to his mom. He promised his mom that he would never do this again.

11.
    (A) while   (B) as
    (C) by   (D) but

12.
    (A) but   (B) while
    (C) since   (D) before

13.
    (A) but   (B) because
    (C) while   (D) as

14.
    (A) but   (B) while
    (C) and   (D) after

15.
    (A) but   (B) as
    (C) if   (D) so

16.
    (A) and   (B) but
    (C) as   (D) so

17.
    (A) so   (B) as
    (C) and   (D) or

18.
    (A) because   (B) and
    (C) but   (D) as

19.
    (A) and   (B) so
    (C) but   (D) while

20.
    (A) since   (B) and
    (C) so   (D) if

21.
    (A) and   (B) so
    (C) as   (D) because

22.
    (A) so   (B) before
    (C) since   (D) but

23.
    (A) as   (B) while
    (C) when   (D) So

24.
    (A) but   (B) because
    (C) If   (D) And

25.
    (A) and   (B) so
    (C) before   (D) since

1.	Ⓐ Ⓑ Ⓒ Ⓓ	6.	Ⓐ Ⓑ Ⓒ Ⓓ	11.	Ⓐ Ⓑ Ⓒ Ⓓ	16	Ⓐ Ⓑ Ⓒ Ⓓ	21.	Ⓐ Ⓑ Ⓒ Ⓓ
2.	Ⓐ Ⓑ Ⓒ Ⓓ	7.	Ⓐ Ⓑ Ⓒ Ⓓ	12.	Ⓐ Ⓑ Ⓒ Ⓓ	17.	Ⓐ Ⓑ Ⓒ Ⓓ	22.	Ⓐ Ⓑ Ⓒ Ⓓ
3.	Ⓐ Ⓑ Ⓒ Ⓓ	8.	Ⓐ Ⓑ Ⓒ Ⓓ	13.	Ⓐ Ⓑ Ⓒ Ⓓ	18.	Ⓐ Ⓑ Ⓒ Ⓓ	23.	Ⓐ Ⓑ Ⓒ Ⓓ
4.	Ⓐ Ⓑ Ⓒ Ⓓ	9.	Ⓐ Ⓑ Ⓒ Ⓓ	14.	Ⓐ Ⓑ Ⓒ Ⓓ	19.	Ⓐ Ⓑ Ⓒ Ⓓ	24.	Ⓐ Ⓑ Ⓒ Ⓓ
5.	Ⓐ Ⓑ Ⓒ Ⓓ	10.	Ⓐ Ⓑ Ⓒ Ⓓ	15.	Ⓐ Ⓑ Ⓒ Ⓓ	20.	Ⓐ Ⓑ Ⓒ Ⓓ	25.	Ⓐ Ⓑ Ⓒ Ⓓ

TENSES

LEARNING OBJECTIVES

➤ Different types of tenses

PRACTICE EXERCISE

I. Complete each sentence below with the future tense form of the verb given in brackets.

1. I _________ my test on time. (complete)

2. We _________ in the summer. (swim)

3. The man _____________ his lawn in the afternoon. (water)

4. The girls _____________ with each other on the weekend. (play)

5. The scientists _____________ the outcome of the experiment. (predict)

6. I _____________ as many books as I can this summer. (read)

7. The students _____________ for the final exam. (study)

8. The dog _____ its tail for food. (wag)

9. The players _____ for their teammate. (pray)

10. My mother _____________ me up from school. (pick)

II. Read the following sentences and fill in the blanks with the correct simple present tenses. Choose answers from the options given below

11. Kunal _________ very fast. He clock every day.
    (A) runs   (B) running
    (C) run   (D) ran

12. I _________ school at 7 o clock everyday.
    (A) goes to   (B) go to
    (C) going to   (D) go

13. He _________ the poem so well that he always wins in the competition.
    (A) recited   (B) recite
    (C) recites   (D) reciting

14. He _________ to collect stamps.
    (A) likes   (B) liked
    (C) like   (D) liking

15. My mother is a great cook, she _________ good food.
    (A) cooked   (B) cook
    (C) cooks   (D) cooking

16. He _________ up early in the morning.
    (A) get   (B) got
    (C) getting   (D) gets

17. The President of India _________ in the Rashtrapati Bhawan.
    (A) lives   (B) live
    (C) living   (D) lived

18. He _________ very good Spanish.
    (A) speaks   (B) spoke
    (C) speaking   (D) speaks

19. Shreyas _________ to eat ice cream even during winters.

(A) like   (B) liked
(C) liking   (D) likes

20. He ________ cricket in the park.
    (A) plays   (B) played
    (C) playing   (D) play

21. He ________ his own football to play with us.
    (A) gets   (B) getting
    (C) got   (D) get

22. You will not understand, they ________ Italian.
    (A) speak   (B) spoke
    (C) speaking   (D) speaks

23. We all ________ watching movies.
    (A) enjoy   (B) enjoys
    (C) enjoying   (D) D)enjoyed

24. My father ________ for office at 8' in the morning.
    (A) leaves   (B) leaving
    (C) left   (D) leave

25. He ________ his own clothes, his mother does not wash his clothes.
    (A) washed   (B) washes
    (C) wash   (D) washing

26. His father ________ not let him play chess.
    (A) do   (B) did
    (C) does   (D) doing

27. He ________ quite well, he is a great singer.
    (A) sang   (B) sings
    (C) singing   (D) sing

28. They all ________ to the Church every Sunday.
    (A) gone   (B) go
    (C) going   (D) goes

29. We should ________ our teeth before going to bed.
    (A) brush   (B) brushed
    (C) brushing   (D) brushes

30. Mr. Tod has a white cap and he ________ that cap.
    (A) loves   (B) loved
    (C) love   (D) loving

HOTS (ACHIEVERS SECTION)

Write the simple past tense for the following irregular verbs.

31. Teach   _____________

32. Give   _____________

33. Read   _____________

34. Bring   _____________

35. Eat   _____________

———Darken Your Choice with HB Pencil———

1. Ⓐ Ⓑ Ⓒ Ⓓ	8. Ⓐ Ⓑ Ⓒ Ⓓ	15. Ⓐ Ⓑ Ⓒ Ⓓ	22 Ⓐ Ⓑ Ⓒ Ⓓ	29. Ⓐ Ⓑ Ⓒ Ⓓ
2. Ⓐ Ⓑ Ⓒ Ⓓ	9. Ⓐ Ⓑ Ⓒ Ⓓ	16. Ⓐ Ⓑ Ⓒ Ⓓ	23. Ⓐ Ⓑ Ⓒ Ⓓ	30. Ⓐ Ⓑ Ⓒ Ⓓ
3. Ⓐ Ⓑ Ⓒ Ⓓ	10. Ⓐ Ⓑ Ⓒ Ⓓ	17. Ⓐ Ⓑ Ⓒ Ⓓ	24. Ⓐ Ⓑ Ⓒ Ⓓ	31. Ⓐ Ⓑ Ⓒ Ⓓ
4. Ⓐ Ⓑ Ⓒ Ⓓ	11. Ⓐ Ⓑ Ⓒ Ⓓ	18. Ⓐ Ⓑ Ⓒ Ⓓ	25. Ⓐ Ⓑ Ⓒ Ⓓ	32. Ⓐ Ⓑ Ⓒ Ⓓ
5. Ⓐ Ⓑ Ⓒ Ⓓ	12. Ⓐ Ⓑ Ⓒ Ⓓ	19. Ⓐ Ⓑ Ⓒ Ⓓ	26. Ⓐ Ⓑ Ⓒ Ⓓ	33. Ⓐ Ⓑ Ⓒ Ⓓ
6. Ⓐ Ⓑ Ⓒ Ⓓ	13. Ⓐ Ⓑ Ⓒ Ⓓ	20. Ⓐ Ⓑ Ⓒ Ⓓ	27. Ⓐ Ⓑ Ⓒ Ⓓ	34. Ⓐ Ⓑ Ⓒ Ⓓ
7. Ⓐ Ⓑ Ⓒ Ⓓ	14. Ⓐ Ⓑ Ⓒ Ⓓ	21. Ⓐ Ⓑ Ⓒ Ⓓ	28. Ⓐ Ⓑ Ⓒ Ⓓ	35. Ⓐ Ⓑ Ⓒ Ⓓ

CONTRACTIONS AND WORD ORDER

PRACTICE EXERCISE

I. Choose the contracted form of the following:

1. Are not
   - (a) Are'not
   - (b) Are'nt
   - (c) Aren't
   - (d) Ar'not

2. They are
   - (a) There're
   - (b) They're
   - (C) The're
   - (d) There'are

3. Do not
   - (a) Don't
   - (b) Do'not
   - (C) Do'nt
   - (d) Dont'

4. Let us
   - (a) Let'us
   - (b) Le'tus
   - (c) Lets'
   - (d) Let's

5. There are
   - (A) There're
   - (b) They'are
   - (c) There'are
   - (d) Therere'

6. Does not
   - (a) Does'not
   - (b) Doesn't'
   - (c) Does'nt
   - (D) Doesn't

7. I am
   - (a) I'am
   - (B) I'm
   - (C) Im'
   - (d) Iam'

8. Have not
   - (a) Have'not
   - (b) Have'nt
   - (c) Have't
   - (D) Haven't

9. He would
   - (A) He'wud
   - (B) He'would
   - (C) He'd
   - (D) He'wd

10. He will
    - (A) He'll
    - (B) He'will
    - (C) He'ill
    - (D) Hew'll

II. Direction for 1 to 8: Given below are the names of some fruits but the letters have been jumbled. Arrange these letters to form the names of the fruits. Then tick the correct options.

11. PGERAS
    - (A) Gpares
    - (B) Grapes
    - (C) Graeps
    - (D) Grasep

12. APYPAA
    - (A) Papaay
    - (B) Papyaa
    - (C) Papaya
    - (D) Paapya

13. KIIW
    - (A) Kiwi
    - (B) I wik
    - (C) Wiki
    - (D) wiik

14. ANGROE
    - (A) Oraeng
    - (B) Orange
    - (C) Ornage
    - (D) Onagre

15. AVAUG
    - (A) Gauva
    - (B) Guvaa
    - (C) Guava
    - (D) Gaavu

16. EHYCLE
    (A) Lyeech   (B) Lychee
    (C) Lycehe   (D) Leechy
17. TUNOOCC
    (A) Coocnut   (B) cocotun
    (C) Nocotuc   (D) coconut
18. LAPEP
    (A) Appel   (B) Apple
    (C) Alppe   (D) Eppal

III. Direction for 9 to 16 : Make meaningful words from the following jumbled letters and then tick the correct options.

19. NTBOKOE
    (A) Noetbook   (B) Nootboke
    (C) Notebook   (D) Tonebook
20. POHEN
    (A) Phoen   (B) Phone
    (C) Pheno   (D) Pheon
21. ORHN
    (A) Horn
    (B) Honr
    (C) Rohn
    (D) Nohr
22. NADII
    (A) Indai
    (B) India
    (C) linda
    (D) Inida
23. CHOSLO
    (A) Shcool
    (B) School
    (C) Schloo
    (D) Cshool
24. ALFBOUF
    (A) Buffaol
    (B) Buffalo
    (C) Bufaflo
    (D) Boffalu

25. RECAM
    (A) Craem
    (B) Crema
    (C) Crame
    (D) Cream
26. IOLN
    (A) Loni
    (B) Inol
    (C) Lion
    (D) Niol

IV. Direction 17 to 20: Andy was writing the spellings of some vegetables. His little brother jumbled up the spellings. Help Andy in selecting the correct spellings by ticking the right options from the following:

27. NJALRIB
    (A) Brinjia
    (B) Brinjal
    (C) Brinlaj
    (D) Binjral
28. EPSA
    (A) Apse
    (B) Paes
    (C) Psea
    (D) Peas
29. RAGCIL
    (A) Gralic
    (B) Garcil
    (C) Garlic
    (D) Garcli
30. URNITP
    (A) Tunrip
    (B) Turnip
    (C) Trunip
    (D) Truinp

Directions: Read the passage carefully and replace the words with their contractions from the options given below.

Reema decided to go out with her school friends. (31) They will go out on Sunday. (32) It is great fun to go for an outing with them. (33) They had all decided to watch a movie together. Given a choice Reema (34) would not have watched a movie. (35) She is not very fond of watching movies. But since all her friends were going she would also go. She knew quite well that it will be of great fun. Going out with friends is always exciting. They ore your greatest treasures. After the movie they will have food outside. It is going to be a great day!

31.
(A) theyl'l   (B) they'll
(C) the'yll   (D) they'll'

32.
(A) it's   (B) its'
(C) i'ts   (D) its

33.
(A) they'd   (B) they'de
(C) they'ed   (D) theyd'

34.
(A) wouldn't   (B) won't
(C) would'nt   (D) will'nt

35.
(A) she's   (B) she'se
(C) she'is   (D) shoes

Darken Your Choice with HB Pencil

1.	A B C D	8.	A B C D	15.	A B C D	22	A B C D	29.	A B C D
2.	A B C D	9.	A B C D	16.	A B C D	23.	A B C D	30.	A B C D
3.	A B C D	10.	A B C D	17.	A B C D	24.	A B C D	31.	A B C D
4.	A B C D	11.	A B C D	18.	A B C D	25.	A B C D	32.	A B C D
5.	A B C D	12.	A B C D	19.	A B C D	26.	A B C D	33.	A B C D
6.	A B C D	13.	A B C D	20.	A B C D	27.	A B C D	34.	A B C D
7.	A B C D	14.	A B C D	21.	A B C D	28.	A B C D	35.	A B C D

PRACTICE EXERCISE

Learning to read and comprehend text is a major milestone in a child's life. The majority of children are reading on a basic level before entering the third grade, when comprehending the written word is a necessity.

Here are some tips to read a book with images to help improve the reading comprehension of a child.

Develop Your Child's Reading Comprehension through Illustrations

1. By hearing and seeing a story, children not only utilize multiple learning styles, but they also learn to comprehend words through illustrations. This later develops into the ability to generate images in the mind while reading.

   For example, when a child reads the word "ball," an image of ball is instantly created in his mind. If you were to read the sentence "The girl bounced the ball," you can visualize a girl bouncing a ball.

2. Explain what is happening in the illustrations and point out small details that go with the text that your child may miss. Show your child each of the characters and explain the setting.

3. Allow your child adequate time to view the images and comprehend what is happening in the story.

4. Tell your child that the pictures will help them understand the story and explain the importance of seeing the images in their minds while you are reading the text.

5. Ask your child what they see, hear, smell, taste, and feel as well as what words helped them develop those emotions and images.

6. Over time, increase the amount of text you read before pausing. Eventually you will be able to read an entire book and have your child explain the meaning and story.

7. Ensure to use the books that have illustrations so that you may promote good reading comprehension skills. Developing minds are always eager to learn.

I. Read the passage and fill in the blanks with appropriate word given in the brackets.

Penguins

Penguins are birds that cannot fly. Their wings are called flippers which they use to help them travel up to thirty miles per hour in water. They also use their flippers for balancing as they walk.

Penguins eat fish. They spend most of their time in the water. Penguins lay their eggs and raise their young on land.

There are many different kinds of penguins. Emperor penguins are the largest species of penguin and can grow to be about four feet tall, and weigh about one hundred pounds. Some other well-known penguin species are the King penguins, the Macaroni penguins, and the Adelie penguins.

8. A penguin is a ____________. (bird, reptile, fish)

9. A penguin can swim up to ________ miles per hour. (twenty, thirty, fifty)

10. Penguins like to eat ____________. (pizza, eggs, fish)

11. Penguins spend most of their time in the ________________. (desert, zoo, water)

12. The ______________ penguin is the largest penguin. (Emperor, Macaroni, King)

13. A penguin is a bird that can't ________. (walk, fly, swim)

II. Read the passage and answer the questions that follow.

Superhero Joey

Joey put on his mask.
He flapped his cape in front of the mirror.
This is the best costume, he thought.
I'm sure to win the contest.

Joey skipped downstairs.

"Here I come to rescue you!" Joey shouted.
"Nice costume," said Joey's dad.
"I'm a superhero," said Joey.

"Joey," said Mom, "I need you to watch Mindy at the party."
Joey looked at his little sister. "But Mom, superheroes don't have kid sisters."
"Well this superhero has a sister," said Mom.
"What will Mindy's costume be?" asked Dad.
"I'm not sure," said Mom.
Joey got an idea. "I know!"

Joey took Mindy upstairs to his room.
He dug through his closet.

Joey found his baby blanket.
He put it around Mindy's shoulders.

At the party, Superhero Joey and his sidekick Supergirl Mindy won first prize!

14. Why was Joey dressed like a superhero?

____

15. What was Joey supposed to do at the party?
    (A) fly in the air
    (B) help make the food
    (C) watch his little sister
    (D) clean up
16. Name all four characters in this story.

____

17. When does this story take place?
    (A) at the party
    (B) before the party
    (C) after the party
    (D) at Joey's house
18. What did Joey put on Mindy when he dressed her up as Supergirl?

____

SPOKEN AND WRITTEN EXPRESSION; PUNCTUATION

LEARNING OBJECTIVES

✓ Usage of Different types of Punctuation marks

PRACTICE EXERCISE

I. Match the following sentences with the correct response.

1.	I am so sorry for eating your lunch.	(a)	Hi Geetika. How are you?
2.	Can you give me two stamps?	(b)	The train leaves at 5.
3.	I would like you to meet my dad.	(c)	I am well. How are you?
4.	Are you well, Nipun?	(d)	Yes, I can mend it in an hour.
5.	Would you be able to mend the bike?	(e)	Hello, how do you do?
6.	This is Stuti, she lives here.	(f)	Yes, you can take this bag.
7.	Could you tell me when the train leaves?	(g)	Sorry, I have only 1 stamp.
8.	How are you doing?	(h)	I am well, thank you.
9.	Hi Akash, I am Geetika.	(i)	That's slright, I was not hungry anyway.
10.	May I take this bag?	(j)	Hi Stuti, how are you?

II. Choose the correctly punctuated sentence.

11. (A) My first job in a factory involved the manufacture of escalator handles and ketchup bottle lids.
    (B) My first job in a factory involved the manufacture of escalator handles, and ketchup bottle lids.
    (C) My first job in a factory involved the manufacture of escalator, handles, and ketchup, bottle lids.
    (D) None of these

12. (A) Ms. Kiran has offered to coach the team this year, however, the competition for the job is intense.
    (B) Ms. Kiran has offered to coach the team this year, however the competition for the job is intense.
    (C) Ms. Kiran has offered to coach the team this year; however, the competition for the job is intense.
    (D) None of these

13. (A) Given the hard choices our coach has had to make this year it's no wonder she's decided to retire.
    (B) Given the hard choices our coach has had to make this year, it's no wonder she's decided to retire.
    (C) Given the hard choices, our coach has had to make this year; it's no wonder she's decided to retire.
    (D) None of these

14. (A) Pawan has been too busy to keep up with his courses because he took on too many extracurricular activities.
    (B) Pawan has been too busy to keep up with his courses, because he took on too many extracurricular activities.
    (C) Pawan has been very busy to keep up with his courses; because he took on too many extracurricular activities.
    (D) None of these

15. (A) After studying the problem for several years, the college worked on a plan to address it.
    (B) After studying the problem, for several years the college worked on a plan to address it.
    (C) The college, after studying the problem for several years worked on a plan to address it.
    (D) All three sentences are correctly punctuated with commas.

HOTS (ACHIEVERS SECTION)

Directions: Read the following passage carefully and fill in the blanks with the correct punctuation marks.

Doing little work at home is good for children ___ (16)___ All the children should do some work at home ___(17)___ Even if children do little work like, keeping their toys after playing ___(18)___ the can be of great help to parents ___(19)___ Children become responsible if they start doing little work at home ___(20)___ It is important that children become responsible ___ (21)___ They can do little work like dress themselves up and keep their clothes in place ___(22)___ The children will love to help their parents with washing the cars ___(23)___ going for grocery shopping or may be preparing their breakfast ___(24)___ Helping your parents can be a daily exercise too ___(25)___.

16. (A) .   (B) ,
    (C) !   (D) ?

17. (A) !   (B) ,
    (C) .   (D) ?

18. (A) .   (B) ,
    (C) !   (D) ?

19. (A) . (B) ,
   (C) ! (D) ?

20. (A) . (B) ,
   (C) ! (D) ?

21. (A) . (B) ,
   (C) ! (D) ?

22. (A) . (B) ,
   (C) ! (D) ?

23. (A) . (B) ,
   (C) ! (D) ?

24. (A) . (B) ,
   (C) ! (C) ?

25. (A) . (B) ,
   (C) ! (D) ?

1.	Ⓐ Ⓑ Ⓒ Ⓓ	6.	Ⓐ Ⓑ Ⓒ Ⓓ	11.	Ⓐ Ⓑ Ⓒ Ⓓ	16	Ⓐ Ⓑ Ⓒ Ⓓ	21.	Ⓐ Ⓑ Ⓒ Ⓓ
2.	Ⓐ Ⓑ Ⓒ Ⓓ	7.	Ⓐ Ⓑ Ⓒ Ⓓ	12.	Ⓐ Ⓑ Ⓒ Ⓓ	17.	Ⓐ Ⓑ Ⓒ Ⓓ	22.	Ⓐ Ⓑ Ⓒ Ⓓ
3.	Ⓐ Ⓑ Ⓒ Ⓓ	8.	Ⓐ Ⓑ Ⓒ Ⓓ	13.	Ⓐ Ⓑ Ⓒ Ⓓ	18.	Ⓐ Ⓑ Ⓒ Ⓓ	23.	Ⓐ Ⓑ Ⓒ Ⓓ
4.	Ⓐ Ⓑ Ⓒ Ⓓ	9.	Ⓐ Ⓑ Ⓒ Ⓓ	14.	Ⓐ Ⓑ Ⓒ Ⓓ	19.	Ⓐ Ⓑ Ⓒ Ⓓ	24.	Ⓐ Ⓑ Ⓒ Ⓓ
5.	Ⓐ Ⓑ Ⓒ Ⓓ	10.	Ⓐ Ⓑ Ⓒ Ⓓ	15.	Ⓐ Ⓑ Ⓒ Ⓓ	20.	Ⓐ Ⓑ Ⓒ Ⓓ	25.	Ⓐ Ⓑ Ⓒ Ⓓ

OLYMPIAD WORKBOOK (IEO) CLASS— 2

MODEL TEST PAPER

1. Pick out the preposition of time from the following:
   (A) By   (B) Across
   (C) Inside   (D) Towards

2. Pick out the correct past tense of 'bake' from the following options:
   (A) Baken   (B) Baking
   (C) Bakes   (D) Baked

3. Pick out the modal from the follow-ing words:
   (A) By   (B) Should
   (C) Praying   (D) Across

4. Pick out the adverb of time from the following words:
   (A) Mainly   (B) Daily
   (C) Quickly   (D) Sadly

5. What is the past tense of the irregular verb 'keep'?
   (A) Keeping   (B) Will keep
   (C) Shall keep   (D) Kept

6. Pick out the reflexive pronoun from the following words:
   (A) Sourabh   (B) He
   (C) Each other   (D) Himself

7. Spot the odd one out:
   (A) Coffee table   (B) Shawl
   (C) Bed   (D) Stool

8. Pick the correct pair:
   (A) Fall – Falled   (B) Give – Gave
   (C) Hang – Hangged   (D) Do – Doed

9. Which of the following cannot be worn in the summer?
   (A) Sweater   (B) Tee shirt
   (C) Skirt   (D) Shorts

10. Pick out the correct collocation for the word 'make':
    (A) Make lunch   (B) Make room
    (C) Make song   (D) Make in India

11. What is the future tense of 'go' ?
    (A) Going   (B) Went
    (C) Goes   (D) Will go

12. Spot the incorrect pair:
    (A) Snake – brood   (B) Bee – colony
    (C) Owl – farm   (D) Lion – pride

13. What is the home of a dog called?
    (A) Shed   (B) Kennel
    (C) Pig-sty   (D) Flock

14. Pick out the correct auxiliary verb from the following words:
    (A) Have   (B) Play
    (C) Dance   (D) Music

15. Which emotion would you associate with a gift?
    (A) Excitement   (B) Sadness
    (C) Anxiety   (D) Guilt

16. Spot the incorrect pair:
    (A) Dog – bitch   (B) Rabbit – doe
    (C) Bull – cow   (D) Sheep – sow

17. Pick out the correct collocation for the word 'do':
    (A) Do not sit there   (B) Do nothing
    (C) Do done   (D) Do it!

18. Pick out the indefinite pronoun from the following words:
    (A) Anyone   (B) Itself
    (C) They   (D) Him

19. Choose the correct pair:
   (A) Pay – Paid
   (B) Put – Putted
   (C) Make – Maked
   (D) Hit – Hitted

20. Pick the auxiliary verb from the following words:
   (A) Walk (B) Sleep
   (C) Have (D) Cook

21. Which modal is used when you give advice to someone?
   (A) Would (B) Can
   (C) Could (D) Should

22. Spot the odd one out:
   (A) Table cloth (B) Soap
   (C) Blankets (D) Towels

23. Pick out the correct clothes for rains:
   (A) Muffler (B) Dress
   (C) Jackets (D) Raincoat

24. Pick the odd one out:
   (A) Raincoat (B) Sweater
   (C) Muffler (D) Sadness

25. Spot the incorrect pair:
   (A) Bear – cub (B) Sheep – lamb
   (C) Bee – owlet (D) Ox – calf

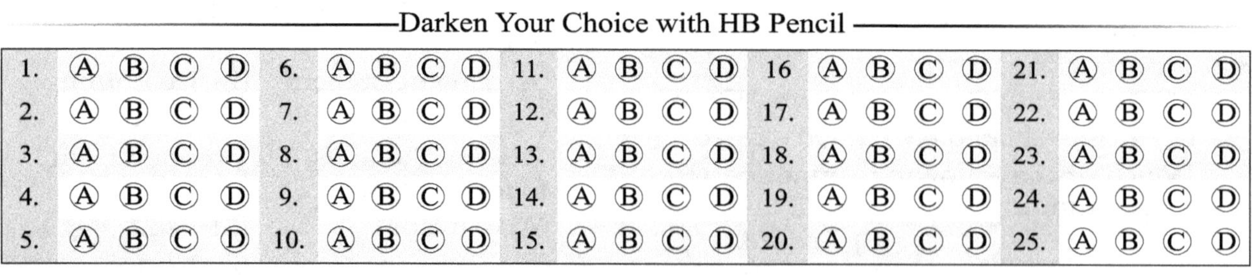

1.	Ⓐ Ⓑ Ⓒ Ⓓ	6.	Ⓐ Ⓑ Ⓒ Ⓓ	11.	Ⓐ Ⓑ Ⓒ Ⓓ	16	Ⓐ Ⓑ Ⓒ Ⓓ	21.	Ⓐ Ⓑ Ⓒ Ⓓ
2.	Ⓐ Ⓑ Ⓒ Ⓓ	7.	Ⓐ Ⓑ Ⓒ Ⓓ	12.	Ⓐ Ⓑ Ⓒ Ⓓ	17.	Ⓐ Ⓑ Ⓒ Ⓓ	22.	Ⓐ Ⓑ Ⓒ Ⓓ
3.	Ⓐ Ⓑ Ⓒ Ⓓ	8.	Ⓐ Ⓑ Ⓒ Ⓓ	13.	Ⓐ Ⓑ Ⓒ Ⓓ	18.	Ⓐ Ⓑ Ⓒ Ⓓ	23.	Ⓐ Ⓑ Ⓒ Ⓓ
4.	Ⓐ Ⓑ Ⓒ Ⓓ	9.	Ⓐ Ⓑ Ⓒ Ⓓ	14.	Ⓐ Ⓑ Ⓒ Ⓓ	19.	Ⓐ Ⓑ Ⓒ Ⓓ	24.	Ⓐ Ⓑ Ⓒ Ⓓ
5.	Ⓐ Ⓑ Ⓒ Ⓓ	10.	Ⓐ Ⓑ Ⓒ Ⓓ	15.	Ⓐ Ⓑ Ⓒ Ⓓ	20.	Ⓐ Ⓑ Ⓒ Ⓓ	25.	Ⓐ Ⓑ Ⓒ Ⓓ

OLYMPIAD WORKBOOK (IEO) CLASS— 2

HINTS AND SOLUTIONS

1. PICTURE QUIZ

Answer Key

1. (A)	2. (A)	3. (B)	4. (D)	5. (A)	6. (C)	7. (C)	8. (A)	9. (D)	10. (D)
11. (D)	12. (C)	13. (A)	14. (C)	15. (C)	16. (C)	17. (B)	18. (B)	19. (D)	20. (A)

HOTS (ACHIEVERS SECTION)

21. (C)	22. (A)	23. (A)	24. (A)	

2. A WORLD OF WORDS

Answer Key

I				
1. (C)	2. (D)	3. (B)	4. (B)	5. (A)

II									
6. (D)	7. (C)	8. (A)	9. (D)	10. (C)	11. (C)	12. (D)	13. (D)	14. (B)	15. (C)

III							
16. Happy/Excited	17. Disappointed	18. Shocked	19. Guilty	20. Scared	21. Sad	22. Frustrated	23. Confused
24. Happy/Excited	25. Relieved	26. Disgusted	27. Sleepy	28. Bored	29. Angry	30. Guilty	

HOTS (ACHIEVERS SECTION)

IV				
31. Rabbit	32. Sheep	33. Bear	34. Lion	35. Ant

V				
36. Breakfast	37. Lunch	38. Snacks	39. Snacks	40. Breakfast/snacks

VI				
41. Anger	42. Love	43. Sadness	44. Happiness	45. Fear

3. WORD POWER : SYNONYMS AND ANTONYMS

Answer Key

I					
1. (A)	2. (D)	3. (A)	4. (A)	5. (B)	6. (C)

II					
7. (A)	8. (B)	9. (C)	10. (D)	11. (C)	12. (B)

III					
13. (A)	14. (C)	15. (A)			

HOTS (ACHIEVERS SECTION)

16. (C)	17. (A)	18. (B)	19. (B)	20. (A)

4. NOUNS

Answer Key

I									
1. (A)	2. (B)	3. (C)	4. (A)	5. (A)	6. (C)	7. (B)	8. (B)	9. (C)	10. (C)

II									
11. (D)	12. (C)								

III									
13. (B)	14. (B)	15. (B)	16. (A)	17. (A)	18. (A)	19. (C)	20. (B)	21. (A)	22. (A)

IV									
23. (C)	24. (C)	25. (A)	26. (C)	27. (B)	28. (A)	29. (A)	30. (A)		

HOTS (ACHIEVERS SECTION)

31. (B)	32. (B)	33. (B)	34. (C)	35. (C)

Answer Key

I

1. (C)	2. (B)	3. (A)	4. (A)	5. (B)	6. (B)	7. (D)	8. (A)	9. (B)	10. (C)
11. (D)	12. (A)	13. (B)	14. (A)	15. (C)					

II

16. (D)	17. (A)	18. (B)	19. (C)	20. (B)	21. (C)	22. (D)	23. (B)	24. (D)	25. (C)
26. (B)	27. (A)	28. (D)	29. (B)	30. (C)					

HOTS (ACHIEVERS SECTION)

31. Possessive	32. Reflexive	33. Indefinite	34. Relative	35. Demonstrative

6. VERBS

Answer Key

I

1. (B)	2. (B)	3. (A)	4. (C)	5. (A)	6. (C)	7. (D)	8. (C)	9. (A)	10. (B)

II

11. (A)	12. (B)	13. (B)	14. (C)	15. (B)					

III

16. (C)	17. (C)	18. (B)	19. (B)	20. (B)	21. (C)	22. (B)	23. (C)	24. (B)	25. (C)

HOTS (ACHIEVERS SECTION)

26. May	27. Can	28. May	29. Would	30. Should

Answer Key

I

1. (B)	2. (C)	3. (D)	4. (C)	5. (D)	6. (B)	7. (A)	8. (C)	9. (B)	10. (D)
11. (A)	12. (C)	13. (B)	14. (C)	15. (A)	16. (D)	17. (B)	18. (C)	19. (A)	20. (C)

II

21. Tomorrow	22. Always	23. Really	24. Obediently	25. Happily
26. Sometimes	27. On	28. Already	29. Twice	30. Lazily

HOTS (ACHIEVERS SECTION)

31. (C)	32. (C)	33. (D)	34. (A)	35. (A)

Answer Key

I

1. (B)	2. (C)	3. (A)	4. (C)	5. (C)	6. (B)	7. (B)	8. (C)

II

9. (A)	10. (B)	11. (C)	12. (C)	13. (C)	14. (A)	15. (A)

HOTS (ACHIEVERS SECTION)

16. (A)	17. (B)	18. (C)	19. (A)	20. (C)

Answer Key

I

1. (C)	2. (C)	3. (D)	4. (B)	5. (B)	6. (A)	7. (D)	8. (A)	9. (C)	10. (B)
11. (B)	12. (A)	13. (A)	14. (B)	15. (A)	16. (A)	17. (B)	18. (B)	19. (B)	20. (A)

HOTS (ACHIEVERS SECTION)

21. (A)	22. (C)	23. (A)	24. (A)	25. (C)

10. PREPOSITIONS

Answer Key

I					
1. beside		2. after		3. between	

II								
4. in	5. behind	6. between	7. beside	8. near	9. on	10. under		

III									
11. (B)	12. (D)	13. (B)	14. (A)	15. (A)	16. (B)	17. (C)	18. (C)	19. (C)	20. (D)
21. (B)	22. (A)	23. (A)	24. (D)	25. (B)	26. (D)	27. (A)	28. (B)	29. (B)	30. (B)

HOTS (ACHIEVERS SECTION)

31. (C)	32. (B)	33. (B)	34. (A)	35. (C)

11. CONJUNCTIONS

Answer Key

1. (B)	2. (B)	3. (A)	4. (A)	5. (D)	6. (A)	7. (B)	8. (B)	9. (A)	10. (A)

HOTS (ACHIEVERS SECTION)

11. (D)	12. (A)	13. (C)	14. (C)	15. (A)	16. (D)	17. (C)	18. (C)	19. (A)	20. (B)
21. (C)	22. (A)	23. (A)	24. (D)	25. (B)					

12. TENSES

Answer Key

I									
1. shall complete	2. shall swim	3. will water	4. will play	5. will predict	6. shall read	7. will study	8. will wag	9. will pray	10. will pick

II									
11. (B)	12. (D)	13. (B)	14. (A)	15. (A)	16. (B)	17. (C)	18. (C)	19. (C)	20. (D)
21. (B)	22. (A)	23. (A)	24. (D)	25. (B)	26. (D)	27. (A)	28. (B)	29. (B)	30. (B)

31. Taught	32. Gave	33. Read	34. Brought	35. Ate

13. CONTRACTIONS AND WORD ORDER

Answer Key

I

1. (C)	2. (B)	3. (A)	4. (D)	5. (A)	6. (D)	7. (B)	8. (D)	9. (C)	10. (A)

II

11. (B)	12. (C)	13. (A)	14. (B)	15. (C)	16. (B)	17. (D)	18. (B)	19. (C)	20. (B)
21. (A)	22. (B)	23. (B)	24. (B)	25. (D)	26. (C)	27. (B)	28. (D)	29. (C)	30. (B)

HOTS (ACHIEVERS SECTION)

31. (B)	32. (A)	33. (A)	34. (A)	35. (A)

14. COMPREHENSION

Answer Key

I

1. birds	2. thirty	3. fish	4. water	5. emperor	6. fly			

II

7. Because he was going to enter a costume contest.	8. (C) watch his little sister
9. Joey, Joey's mom, Joey's dad, and his little sister (Mindy)	10. (B) before the party
11. He put his old baby blanket around Mindy.	

Answer Key

I

1. i	2. g	3. e	4. h	5. d	6. j	7. b	8. c	9. a	10. f

II

11. (A)	12. (C)	13. (B)	14. (A)	15. (A)					

HOTS (ACHIEVERS SECTION)

16. (A)	17. (A)	18. (B)	19. (A)	20. (A)	21. (A)	22. (A)	23. (B)	24. (A)	25. (A)

MODEL TEST PAPER

Answer Key

1. (A)	2. (D)	3. (B)	4. (B)	5. (D)	6. (D)	7. (B)	8. (B)	9. (A)	10. (B)
11. (D)	12. (C)	13. (B)	14. (A)	15. (A)	16. (D)	17. (B)	18. (A)	19. (A)	20. (C)
21. (D)	22. (B)	23. (D)	24. (D)	25. (C)					

SAMPLE OMR ANSWER SHEET

1. STUDENT NAME (IN ENGLISH CAPITAL LETTERS ONLY)

Students must write and darken the respective circles completely using HB Pencil only. Othewise their Answer Sheets will not be evaluated.

PERSONAL DETAILS

2. SCHOOL CODE

3. CLASS

4. SECTION

5. ROLL NO.

6. QUESTION PAPER SET

A ○
B ○
C ○
D ○

7. MOBILE NUMBER

8. GENDER

MALE ○

FEMALE ○

9. STREAM
(Only for Class XI and XII Students)

MATHEMATICS ○
BIOLOGY ○
OTHERS ○

MARK YOUR ANSWERS

1.	Ⓐ Ⓑ Ⓒ Ⓓ				26.	Ⓐ Ⓑ Ⓒ Ⓓ			
2.	Ⓐ Ⓑ Ⓒ Ⓓ				27.	Ⓐ Ⓑ Ⓒ Ⓓ			
3.	Ⓐ Ⓑ Ⓒ Ⓓ				28.	Ⓐ Ⓑ Ⓒ Ⓓ			
4.	Ⓐ Ⓑ Ⓒ Ⓓ				29.	Ⓐ Ⓑ Ⓒ Ⓓ			
5.	Ⓐ Ⓑ Ⓒ Ⓓ				30.	Ⓐ Ⓑ Ⓒ Ⓓ			
6.	Ⓐ Ⓑ Ⓒ Ⓓ				31.	Ⓐ Ⓑ Ⓒ Ⓓ			
7.	Ⓐ Ⓑ Ⓒ Ⓓ				32.	Ⓐ Ⓑ Ⓒ Ⓓ			
8.	Ⓐ Ⓑ Ⓒ Ⓓ				33.	Ⓐ Ⓑ Ⓒ Ⓓ			
9.	Ⓐ Ⓑ Ⓒ Ⓓ				34.	Ⓐ Ⓑ Ⓒ Ⓓ			
10.	Ⓐ Ⓑ Ⓒ Ⓓ				35.	Ⓐ Ⓑ Ⓒ Ⓓ			
11.	Ⓐ Ⓑ Ⓒ Ⓓ				36.	Ⓐ Ⓑ Ⓒ Ⓓ			
12.	Ⓐ Ⓑ Ⓒ Ⓓ				37.	Ⓐ Ⓑ Ⓒ Ⓓ			
13.	Ⓐ Ⓑ Ⓒ Ⓓ				38.	Ⓐ Ⓑ Ⓒ Ⓓ			
14.	Ⓐ Ⓑ Ⓒ Ⓓ				39.	Ⓐ Ⓑ Ⓒ Ⓓ			
15.	Ⓐ Ⓑ Ⓒ Ⓓ				40.	Ⓐ Ⓑ Ⓒ Ⓓ			
16.	Ⓐ Ⓑ Ⓒ Ⓓ				41.	Ⓐ Ⓑ Ⓒ Ⓓ			
17.	Ⓐ Ⓑ Ⓒ Ⓓ				42.	Ⓐ Ⓑ Ⓒ Ⓓ			
18.	Ⓐ Ⓑ Ⓒ Ⓓ				43.	Ⓐ Ⓑ Ⓒ Ⓓ			
19.	Ⓐ Ⓑ Ⓒ Ⓓ				44.	Ⓐ Ⓑ Ⓒ Ⓓ			
20.	Ⓐ Ⓑ Ⓒ Ⓓ				45.	Ⓐ Ⓑ Ⓒ Ⓓ			
21.	Ⓐ Ⓑ Ⓒ Ⓓ				46.	Ⓐ Ⓑ Ⓒ Ⓓ			
22.	Ⓐ Ⓑ Ⓒ Ⓓ				47.	Ⓐ Ⓑ Ⓒ Ⓓ			
23.	Ⓐ Ⓑ Ⓒ Ⓓ				48.	Ⓐ Ⓑ Ⓒ Ⓓ			
24.	Ⓐ Ⓑ Ⓒ Ⓓ				49.	Ⓐ Ⓑ Ⓒ Ⓓ			
25.	Ⓐ Ⓑ Ⓒ Ⓓ				50.	Ⓐ Ⓑ Ⓒ Ⓓ			

Signature of the Student & Date of Examination	Signature of the Invigilator & Date of Examination

V&S Publishers, F-2/16 Ansari Road, Daryaganj, New Delhi-110002, ☎ 011-23240026-27
✉ info@vspublishers.com, 🌐 www.vspublishers.com